Our Changing World

THE TIMELINE LIBRARY

THE HISTORY OF THE POST OFFICE

BY BARBARA A. SOMERVILL

▸ 1918
The first official U.S. airmail service begins.

We use
AIR MAIL
for
important
correspondence
Air mail saves a day
Issued by the COLONIAL AIR TRANSPORT, INC.

▴ 1775
The Continental Congress chooses Benjamin Franklin as the first postmaster general.

▴ 1860
Sending letters by Pony Express costs $5 per 0.5 ounces (14 g).

A.D. 1750 | 1800 | 1850 | 1900 | 1950 | 2000

Content Adviser: Nancy Pope, Curator, National Postal Museum, Washington, D.C.

THE CHILD'S WORLD® • CHANHASSEN, MINNESOTA

Published in the United States of America by The Child's World®
PO Box 326 • Chanhassen, MN 55317-0326 • 800-599-READ • www.childsworld.com

ACKNOWLEDGMENTS

The Child's World®: Mary Berendes, Publishing Director

Editorial Directions, Inc.: E. Russell Primm, Editorial Director; Katie Marsico, Managing Editor and Line Editor; Judith Shiffer, Assistant Editor; Rory Mabin and Caroline Wood, Editorial Assistants; Susan Hindman, Copy Editor; Jennifer Martin, Proofreader; Judith Frisbee, Peter Garnham, Olivia Nellums, Chris Simms, and Stephen Carl Wender, Fact Checkers; Tim Griffin/IndexServ, Indexer; Cian Loughlin O'Day, Photo Researcher; Linda S. Koutris, Photo Selector

The Design Lab: Kathleen Petelinsek, Design and Art Production

PHOTOS

Cover/frontispiece: left—The Granger Collection; center—Craig Aurness/Corbis; right—Swim Ink 2, LLC/Corbis.

Interior: 5—Peter Beck/Corbis; 6, 9, 11, 12, 15, 19—The Granger Collection; 8—Bettmann/Corbis; 17—Hulton|Archive/Kean Collection/Getty Images; 23—Andre Jenny/Alamy Images; 25—Bob Riha Jr./AP Photo; 26—Jose Luis Peleaz Inc./Corbis; 27—Warner Bros./Getty Images; 28—Christophe Calais/In Visu/Corbis; 29—Harry V. Reidy/Alamy Images.

REGISTRATION

LIBRARY OF CONGRESS CATALOGING-IN-PUBLICATION DATA

Somervill, Barbara A.
The history of the post office / by Barbara Somervill.
p. cm. — (The timeline library)
Includes index.
ISBN 1-59296-441-9 (library bound : alk. paper)
1. Postal service—History—Juvenile literature. I. Title. II. Our changing world—the timeline library.
HE6078.S66 2006
383'.49—dc22 2005024778

TABLE OF CONTENTS

INTRODUCTION

THE STAMP COLLECTOR

The mailman delivered a package addressed to Kazumi. It was from Great Uncle Koji.

"It's an album," Kazumi grumbled, "filled with old stamps."

"Oh," said Papa. "They are not just old stamps. Koji is a philatelist."

"I thought he lived in San Francisco, not Philadelphia," said Kazumi.

"I said *philatelist,* Kazumi." Papa pronounced each syllable carefully. "Fill-AH-tell-ist. Uncle Koji is a stamp collector."

Papa read the letter that came with the album. "Uncle Koji is sending an album to each child in the family. He says to use the stamps to pay for your college education."

Kazumi laughed. As if a twenty-four-cent stamp could pay for college. Papa shook his head. "Kazumi, some of these stamps might be worth a lot of money. Let's look them up on the Internet."

The Internet search turned up quite a surprise. The **mint condition** red lilac George Washington twenty-four-cent stamp was worth $895. The orange Benjamin Franklin stamp had a value of $800. And a ninety-cent blue George Washington had a price tag of $1,700.

"I think you'd better write a nice thank-you note to Uncle Koji," said Papa.

"Right," said Kazumi. "And I won't use one of those stamps to mail it."

Certain stamps are worth a great deal of money!

CHAPTER ONE

ANCIENT POST OFFICES

For centuries, sending messages from one place to another was challenging. In Africa, tribes pounded drums to announce strangers in their jungle. In ancient China, a hilltop fire told of an advancing enemy. Smoke signals, bells, and flags delivered news across great distances. It would have been easier to send letters, but there was no mail service.

The earliest records of mail delivery were found in Egypt, from about 2000 B.C. Messengers walked beside the Nile River, carrying messages from the pharaoh in their pouches. The letters contained orders for construction changes to the pharaoh's tomb. These messengers were early mail carriers.

The Chinese also had an early postal service. Records of mail delivery were found scratched on bones and shells from the Shang

ca. 2000 B.C.

Egyptians carry mail by foot along the Nile River.

Acupuncture (left) is first used in China.

dynasty (sixteenth–eleventh centuries B.C.). Only emperors and military officials could use this service. By 900 B.C., the Chinese expanded their mail system. They developed a general postal service for all government material.

By the sixth century B.C., the Persians had developed a postal system using horseback riders and relay stations. Riders carried mail from one station to another, then handed the mail to the next rider. Under King Cyrus the Great, the Persians had two types of mail. One kind involved regular government letters and was carried in oxcarts or by people on foot. Express mail was from kings and top officials and was transported by horseback riders.

DID YOU KNOW?

EARLY PEOPLE TRIED TO KEEP THEIR LETTERS CLEAN, DRY, AND SECRET BY PUTTING THEM IN ENVELOPES. EARLY ENVELOPES WERE MADE FROM CLOTH, ANIMAL HIDES, OR LEAVES. MANY ENVELOPES WERE SEALED WITH WAX. THE BABYLONIANS FOUND AN EVEN BETTER WAY TO KEEP THEIR LETTERS SECRET – THEY BAKED THEM INSIDE CLAY BLOCKS!

900s B.C.

China starts a government-only mail service.

Egyptians perfect the skill of glassmaking.

540 B.C.

Persians develop postal relay stations.

West Africa is influenced by the spread of iron technology.

A.D. 14: CURSUS PUBLICUS

The Romans developed the most extensive postal service for ancient times. They called it *cursus publicus,* or "public course." By A.D. 14, the cursus publicus covered most of Europe and the Middle East, from present-day England to Egypt.

The Roman post carried the news of army victories, new laws, and taxes. The service was quick. Carriers could cover 155 miles (249 kilometers) in twenty-four hours. But when the Roman

The Romans (left) can send mail 155 miles (249 km) in twenty-four hours.

A.D. 14

Tiberius becomes emperor of Rome.

Empire declined, so did the postal service. By the 800s, Roman mail routes had disappeared.

As European countries expanded, government leaders wrote to each other. Military leaders needed to communicate. Business owners and traders wanted to send orders and sell goods in faraway markets. Countries needed a mail system.

During the Middle Ages, sending mail became a business opportunity. Families started private mail services. They hired **couriers** to carry letters and small packages. The Von Taxis family owned the largest postal company. They ran delivery routes in Spain, Germany, Austria, Italy, Hungary, Belgium, the Netherlands, and Luxembourg.

800s

The Roman mail system disappears.

Charlemagne is crowned Emperor of Rome.

1512

The Von Taxis family starts a private postal service in Europe.

Spanish colonies thrive on the Caribbean islands (right).

CHAPTER TWO
THE ROYAL POST

At one time, sending a letter cost nothing. Getting one, however, cost plenty. People who received letters paid the couriers who delivered them. If people had no money, they got no mail.

In the early 1600s, Great Britain began developing regular mail service. By 1626, letters could successfully be sent between London and Plymouth. Within ten years, the British post spread throughout England and was available to all citizens who could afford it. To make sure mail was delivered promptly, British **postmaster** Henry Bishop introduced the postmark in 1661. This mark indicated the date and time a letter was sent.

Postal rates were very expensive. The charge depended on the distance a letter was sent and how many pages the letter contained. Because of the cost,

1626
Great Britain begins mail service between London and Plymouth.
The Dutch buy Manhattan Island for about $24.

1660
English mathematician William Oughtred is born.

most mail came from government offices or businesses.

1775: BENJAMIN FRANKLIN, POSTMASTER GENERAL

British colonists sent mail home to Europe from America. During the 1600s, the British Crown postal service expanded mail service at great cost to the receiver. In 1698, mailing a letter from Boston, Massachusetts, to New York cost twelve **pence.** At that time, most people earned about two British pounds a week (the equivalent of $3.50 today). Since 240 pence equaled one

1661	Henry Bishop introduces the postmark.
	Dutch rule ends in Taiwan.

1698	Mail service (above) from Boston, Massachusetts, to New York costs twelve pence.
	The steam engine is developed by Thomas Savery.

pound, twelve pence amounted to more than 2 percent of a week's income.

In 1774, a printer from Baltimore, Maryland, named William Goddard recommended that the colonies create their own postal service. In 1775, the Continental Congress chose Benjamin Franklin as the first postmaster general. Franklin formed a committee to set up the postal system. By Christmas Day of that year, the British Crown was out of business.

But sending a letter cost even more under the new postal service. In 1776, the Declaration of Independence gave the colonies freedom from British rule. The new United States could

DID YOU KNOW?

On July 26, 1775, the Second Continental Congress established the job of U.S. postmaster general: "A Postmaster General shall be appointed for the Continental Congress, who shall hold his office at Philadelphia, and shall be allowed a salary of 1,000 dollars per annum [year]."

1775

The Continental Congress chooses Benjamin Franklin (left) as the first postmaster general.

American revolutionary Patrick Henry says, "Give me liberty or give me death."

not afford to pay riders to carry mail under the old rates. An express service ran from Cambridge, Massachusetts, to Philadelphia, Pennsylvania. Riders traveled through all types of weather, riding day and night. The cost to send an express post changed with the seasons. Winter rates ran twelve pence per mile. Summer rates were only eight pence per mile.

At this point, stamps did not exist. People still paid to receive letters. To avoid the expensive postage, some people wrote coded messages on the outside of their letters. Recipients looked at the letters, found the messages, and then refused to pay. This was no way to run a post office.

BEN FRANKLIN

BESIDES BEING THE FIRST POSTMASTER GENERAL APPOINTED BY THE CONTINENTAL CONGRESS, BEN FRANKLIN WAS ALSO A PRINTER, WRITER, SCIENTIST, INVENTOR, AND STATESMAN. FRANKLIN PRINTED *POOR RICHARD'S ALMANACK,* WHICH WAS FILLED WITH WISE SAYINGS. "EARLY TO BED AND EARLY TO RISE, MAKES A MAN HEALTHY, WEALTHY, AND WISE" IS ONE OF FRANKLIN'S BEST-KNOWN SAYINGS.

1776

Colonial leaders sign the Declaration of Independence.

CHAPTER THREE
STAMPS, PARCELS, AND AIRMAIL

In 1837, English schoolteacher Rowland Hill came up with an amazing idea. Why not make the sender pay for the mail? Hill had a fascinating way to keep track of paid postage—the **adhesive** postage stamp. In 1840, Hill designed the first British postage stamp, the Penny Black. It featured a picture of Queen Victoria.

People did not use envelopes in those days. They folded up a letter, sealed it with wax, and wrote the address on the outside. Stamps were glued on the corner above the address. Sheets of stamps did not have **perforations** for easy tearing. Postal clerks cut stamps apart with scissors.

Hill wanted a cheap, efficient postal service. Under the new service, sending a letter within England cost one pence per 0.5 ounces (14 grams).

1837

Rowland Hill suggests adhesive postage stamps and prepaid mail service.

Michigan becomes a state.

To prevent people from reusing stamps, the post office placed a mark over the stamp after a letter had been sent. This mark "canceled" the stamp.

Soon other countries began printing adhesive postage stamps. The United States printed its first stamps in 1847. One was a five-cent Ben Franklin stamp. The other was a ten-cent George Washington stamp.

During the 1800s, mail service in the United States crisscrossed a growing nation. Within cities and villages, postal couriers delivered mail on foot. But when letters or parcels traveled from city to city a faster and more efficient delivery system was needed. The post office used stagecoaches, steamboats, and railroad trains for transportation.

DID YOU KNOW?
THE BRITISH GUIANA ONE-CENT MAGENTA STAMP, PRINTED IN 1856, IS THE MOST VALUABLE STAMP IN THE WORLD. ONLY ONE OF THESE STAMPS EXISTS TODAY. IT WAS LAST SOLD IN 1980 FOR $935,000.

1840

The British Royal Post issues its first stamp, the Penny Black (right).

England's Queen Victoria marries Albert of Saxe-Coburg.

> *In a little while all interest was taken up in stretching our necks and watching for the "pony-rider"—the fleet messenger who sped across the continent from St. Joe to Sacramento, carrying letters nineteen hundred miles in eight days! Think of that for perishable horse and human flesh and blood to do! The pony-rider was usually a little bit of a man, brimful of spirit and endurance. No matter what time of the day or night his watch came on, and no matter whether it was winter or summer, raining, snowing, hailing, or sleeting, or whether his "beat" was a level straight road or a crazy trail over mountain crags and precipices, or whether it led through peaceful regions or regions that swarmed with hostile Indians, he must be always ready to leap into the saddle and be off like the wind!*
>
> —From Mark Twain's *Roughing It*

Stagecoaches traveled regular routes, called post roads. Today, the Boston Post Road still exists between New York City and Boston.

1860: THE PONY EXPRESS

A private mail service called the Pony Express got its start in 1860. The Pony Express linked Saint Joseph, Missouri, to Sacramento, California, for eighteen months. It used 183 riders who each typically covered 75 to 100 miles (120 to 160 km) on horseback. Most riders were in their early twenties. Some young riders were in their late teens, and the oldest was forty.

At first, sending letters by Pony Express cost $5 per 0.5 ounces (14 g). These high rates lasted only a short

1856

The world's most valuable stamp, the British Guiana one-cent magenta, is printed.

The Western Union Telegraph Company opens for business.

time. Within the year, the cost of carrying a letter dropped to $1 per ounce.

The owners of the Pony Express hoped to get a government contract to carry the mail. In 1861, however, the Civil War (1861–1865) affected the entire nation. Suddenly, the war demanded all of the government's attention. Then, in October 1861, the telegraph connected the country's East and West coasts. It was cheaper and faster to send a telegram than a letter by Pony Express. The Pony Express came to an end that same month.

1872: MAIL-ORDER GOODS

As the United States pushed west, people in remote areas wanted to purchase the same items that were

1860

The Pony Express (right) gets its start.

Abraham Lincoln is elected the sixteenth U.S. president.

DID YOU KNOW?
IN 1911, THE BRITISH GOVERNMENT TESTED OUT THE IDEA OF AIRMAIL IN ALLAHABAD, INDIA. ON FEBRUARY 18, PILOT HENRI PEQUET TOOK OFF IN A SOMMER **BIPLANE** FOR A 5-MILE (8-KM) TRIP. THE BIPLANE CARRIED 6,500 CARDS AND LETTERS—THE FIRST OFFICIAL AIRMAIL DELIVERY.

available in cities. In 1872, Aaron Montgomery Ward started offering goods that could be ordered by mail. People used his one-page catalog to order everything from boots and buckles to stoves and woolen underwear. Unfortunately, the cost of shipping was high.

In 1913, the U.S. Post Office began parcel service. This meant that people could order goods and have them shipped in small packages through the regular postal service.

1918: OFFICIAL U.S. AIRMAIL

In the United States, airmail and parcel service got their start at about the same time. A test of the airmail system began in 1911 in New York with delivery between Garden City and Mineola. Official airmail—complete with an air-

1872
Aaron Montgomery Ward offers mail-order goods.
Susan B. Anthony illegally votes in a presidential election.

1911
The first airmail delivery takes place in Allahabad, India.
Explorer Roald Amundsen reaches the South Pole.

mail stamp—began in 1918. But that first stamp had a mistake. It featured a plane called the Jenny. On a sheet of 100 stamps, the plane appeared inverted, or upside down. The Inverted Jenny is among the world's most valuable stamps. Its current value stands at about $150,000.

Within two years, the United States tested cross-country airmail. By 1924, **transcontinental** airmail became a standard service. About ten years later, airmail crossed the Atlantic and Pacific oceans. Up until that point, international mail only traveled by ship. A letter took up to four months to be delivered this way. Airmail service between Los Angeles, California, and Tokyo, Japan, cut door-to-door delivery down to three to four days.

1913

The U.S. Post Office offers parcel service.

Henry Ford introduces assembly-line manufacturing.

1918

The first official U.S. airmail service (above) begins.

Revolutionaries execute Czar Nicholas II of Russia and his family.

CHAPTER FOUR

CHANGING THE POSTAL SYSTEM

By the mid-1900s, the amount of mail sorted, shipped, and delivered throughout the United States was massive. The U.S. Post Office dealt with millions of pieces of mail every day. But it was still a hands-on operation.

Mail wasn't just letters. It included magazines and newspapers, ads, bills, bank statements and receipts, checks, postcards, and reminders of dental appointments. Post offices were flooded with mail. Methods of handling mail had not changed in a century. Dealing with the massive amount of mail became impossible.

In 1963, the U.S. Post Office decided to make sorting mail simpler. Every community got a ZIP code. These are five-digit numbers that indicate

1959

The Post Office experiments with mail-by-missile.

Monkeys are sent into space and return unharmed.

the region, state, and town for a particular address. The first digit stands for the general region. The next two digits pinpoint the state and city. The last two digits show the town or neighborhood. Everyone was instructed to include ZIP codes when addressing mail.

During the late 1960s, the Post Office added a number of services and technologies. It introduced mechanical scanners that helped sort mail more quickly. The scanners could read both typed and handwritten ZIP codes. In 1968, a new class of mail called Priority Mail moved letters and packages more quickly and effectively, at a considerably higher price than the standard postage stamp.

DID YOU KNOW?

In 1959, the U.S. Post Office conducted an experiment. It launched 3,000 letters in a guided missile fired from a submarine, the USS *Barbero*. A Post Office representative said, "Before man reaches the moon, mail will be delivered within hours from New York to California, to Britain, to India, or Australia by guided missile mail." Despite this prediction, mail-by-missile never got off the ground.

1963

ZIP codes are introduced.

President John F. Kennedy is assassinated in Dallas, Texas.

SELF-ADHESIVE STAMPS

The first countries to offer self-adhesive stamps were Sierra Leone in 1964 and Tonga and Bhutan in 1969. Up to this point, people used water-activated stamps that they usually licked before pasting onto an envelope. But water-activated stamps didn't work well in Sierra Leone, Tonga, or Bhutan because of these countries' damp climates. Self-adhesive stamps don't need to be licked because they already have a sticky backing. The first U.S. self-stick stamp was the ten-cent Christmas Dove Weathervane, issued in 1974.

1971: THE USPS OPENS FOR BUSINESS

By the late 1960s, the U.S. Post Office had made some improvements, but it still had a long way to go. Its buildings were in bad condition, postal employees were working for low salaries, and an old-fashioned system was still being used to move the mail. At this time, the federal government ran the Post Office. The solution was for the Post Office to run itself. In 1971, the U.S. Post Office Department became a separate company called the U.S. Postal Service (USPS). It was still owned by the federal government, but the USPS mostly managed its own affairs.

The USPS began to rely more and more on automated equipment. Computerized machines read addresses

1971

The USPS opens for business.

Bangladesh declares independence from Pakistan.

and sorted mail. This new technology led to quicker deliveries. The USPS set standards to assure overnight delivery of 95 percent of airmail within 600 miles (966 km) and 95 percent of local stamped mail.

The new USPS also added services. In 1972, people could order stamps by mail instead of buying them at a post office. In 1977, airmail disappeared. Letters still traveled on planes, but people did not have to pay an extra fee for that service. A regular first-class

1977

The USPS introduces Express Mail (right).

Jimmy Carter is sworn in as the thirty-ninth president of the United States.

stamp was enough to send a letter, whether it was being mailed from block to block or state to state. That same year, the USPS began Express Mail. For a higher fee, overnight delivery of a letter or parcel was guaranteed.

Over time, stamps became even easier to buy. Once stamps-by-mail proved successful, the USPS offered stamps-by-phone and, in 1990, Easy Stamps. Easy Stamps allow customers to purchase postage over the computer. The USPS also developed automatic teller machines (ATMs) to sell stamps. People put the coins in one slot, and stamps came out the other.

The 1990s saw a major change in mail delivery. Cheaper long-distance phone plans, fax machines, and

ZIP + 4

The USPS introduced the idea of ZIP+4 in 1983. The last four digits refer to a specific apartment building, city block, street, or rural area.

1983

The USPS introduces ZIP+4.

In France, the AIDS virus is identified.

1990

People use Easy Stamps to buy postage online.

Political Activist Nelson Mandela is released from prison.

e-mail cut the volume of regular mail significantly. Today, companies often send bills online, and people pay their bills the same way. Most companies also offer toll-free phone numbers or Internet Web sites that people can use to place orders for various products.

Not everyone was pleased with how the USPS had changed. Between 1971 and 1992, it had gone from too few employees to too many, and from too little equipment

People can use ATMs (right) to purchase stamps.

1992

Civil war breaks out in Yugoslavia.

to too much. Other problems included its inability to control postage rates and competition from e-mail. In order to survive, the USPS needed to become more efficient. It began to offer even more services online and reduced its workforce by 30,000 people.

The USPS also increased its rates for delivering mail. In 1960, the cost of a first-class stamp was four cents. By 1975, regular stamps cost thirteen cents each. During the 1980s, postage stamps rose from eighteen cents to twenty-five cents. Today, a stamp costs thirty-seven cents. Tomorrow . . . well, it's no wonder most people send e-mail. It's free . . . for now.

1995

AOL, Prodigy, and CompuServe begin providing Internet access (left) to millions of people.

A bomb at the Alfred P. Murrah Federal Building in Oklahoma City, Oklahoma, kills 168 people.

CHAPTER FIVE
THE MAIL OF TOMORROW

By 2001, the USPS faced an increasingly dangerous threat. People were sending letter bombs and mail containing deadly chemicals such as anthrax. Mail had become more than ads, bills, and birthday cards. It was being used as a terrorist weapon. New rules were needed to make mail safer.

Items weighing more than 14 ounces (397 g) can no longer be placed in outside mail drops. Those packages have to be brought inside a post office to mail. Foreign mail and packages are checked carefully to make sure they are safe. For example, mail shipped out of Australia bears a sticker guaranteeing that the sender presented identification to a postal worker.

2003: WHAT MAKES UP MODERN-DAY MAIL

The USPS releases a report on its mail service every year. The 2003 report says

2001

The USPS addresses public safety concerns after mail is increasingly used as a terrorist weapon.

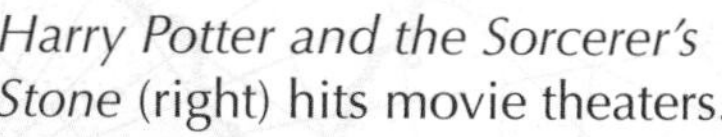

Harry Potter and the Sorcerer's Stone (right) hits movie theaters.

> "If we have learned anything from the financial pressures we are facing, it is that we can no longer rely on past strategies of raising rates for long-term success."
>
> —John Potter, postmaster general (2001–)

that the USPS handled 202.2 billion pieces of mail that year. Most of that mail was letters—meaning actual letters, bills, bill payments, birthday cards, and so on. Other mail categories include newspapers and magazines, ads, packages, and international mail. Compared to previous years, there was a small increase in the amount of packages, standard mail (letters), and international mail sent in 2003.

THE POST OFFICE OF THE FUTURE

The USPS faces a challenging future. As more people take advantage of e-mail and Internet services, there is a continued decrease in mail volume. To survive, the USPS will need to offer better services that people can use more easily.

Perhaps all the post offices of tomorrow will be self-

2003

The USPS delivers 202.2 billion pieces of mail.

The United States invades Iraq (left).

service centers, which have become more common since the 1980s. Or they may become strictly drive-throughs, with postage charged to a credit card. It is possible that the USPS may have to compete with other mail services. The growth of companies such as United Parcel Service (UPS) and Federal Express (FedEx) has proven that private package delivery is a reliable option. These companies don't have to follow the same restrictions and demands as the USPS.

The future of post offices is not clear. But even as times change, one thing remains certain. Nothing can truly replace the joy of getting a letter from a friend or a card from Grandma.

2004

The USPS introduces a self-service center called the Automated Postal Center (right).

A series of terrible hurricanes hit the southern United States.

adhesive (ad-HEE-siv)
An adhesive is a type of glue. Rowland Hill recommended the use of adhesive postage stamps.

biplane (BYE-playn)
A biplane is a type of plane with two pairs of wings that are positioned at different levels, one above the main part of the aircraft and the other beneath it. The first airmail delivery was made with a biplane in 1911.

couriers (KOOR-ee-urz)
Couriers are messengers or message carriers. Couriers on horseback delivered mail during the Middle Ages.

mint condition (MINT kuhn-DISH-uhn)
Something in mint condition is perfect or has never been used. A mint-condition stamp from 1856 is usually worth more than one that was used on a letter.

pence (PENSS)
Pence is a small division of British pounds, much like cents is a division of dollars. In the late 1600s, mailing a letter from Massachusetts to New York cost twelve pence.

perforations (pur-fuh-RAY-shuhnz)
Perforations are a series of small holes that allow something to be torn easily. Early stamps had no perforations and had to be cut apart with scissors.

postmaster (POHST-mass-tuhr)
A postmaster is someone who runs a post office. British postmaster Henry Bishop introduced the postmark.

transcontinental (transs-kon-tuh-NEN-tuhl)
Something that is transcontinental spans a country. Transcontinental airmail was a standard service by 1924.

AT THE LIBRARY

Nonfiction

Anderson, Peter. *The Pony Express.* Danbury, Conn.: Children's Press, 1998.

Lucas, Eileen. *Our Postal System.* Brookfield, Conn.: Millbrook Press, 1999.

Miller, Raymond. *U.S. Stamps: Collecting Guide.* New York: Tangerine Press, 2003.

*Moeller, Jan, and Bill Moeller. *The Pony Express: A Photographic History.* Missoula, Mont.: Mountain Press Publishing, 2003.

*The USPS, William Henderson, James Bruns, and Carl Burcham. *An American Postal Portrait: A Photographic Legacy.* New York: HarperResource, 2000.

Fiction

Lyons, Mary E. *Letters from a Slave Girl: The Story of Harriet Jacobs.* New York: Simon Pulse, 1996.

* *Books marked with a star are challenge reading material for those reading above grade level.*

ON THE WEB

Visit our home page for lots of links about post offices:
http://www.childsworld.com/links

Note to Parents, Teachers, and Librarians:
We routinely check our Web links to make sure they're safe, active sites—so encourage your readers to check them out!

PLACES TO VISIT OR CONTACT

The National Postal Museum
2 Massachusetts Avenue NE
Washington, DC 20002
202/633-5555

Spellman Museum of Stamps and Postal History
235 Wellesley Street at Regis College
Weston, MA 02493
781/768-8367

INDEX

ABOUT THE AUTHOR

Barbara Somervill is the author of many books for children. She loves learning and sees every writing project as a chance to learn new information or gain a new understanding. Ms. Somervill grew up in New York State, but has also lived in Toronto, Canada; Canberra, Australia; California; and South Carolina. She currently lives with her husband in Simpsonville, South Carolina.